ANIMALS
That Change the World!

Elephants

Ashley Lee

Explore other books at:
WWW.ENGAGEBOOKS.COM

VANCOUVER, B.C.

WWW.ENGAGEBOOKS.COM

Elephants: Level 2
Animals That Change the World!
Lee, Ashley 1995 –
Text © 2020 Engage Books
Design © 2020 Engage Books

Edited by: A.R. Roumanis,
Jared Siemens, and Lauren Dick
Design by: A.R. Roumanis

Text set in Arial Regular.
Chapter headings set in Arial Black.

FIRST EDITION / FIRST PRINTING

LIBRARY AND ARCHIVES CANADA CATALOGUING IN PUBLICATION

Title: Elephants: Animals That Change the World Level 2 reader / Ashley Lee
Names: Lee, Ashley, 1995- author

Identifiers: Canadiana (print) 20200308858 | Canadiana (ebook) 20200308866
ISBN 978-1-77437-616-4 (hardcover)
ISBN 978-1-77437-756-7 (softcover)
ISBN 978-1-77437-618-8 (pdf)
ISBN 978-1-77437-619-5 (epub)
ISBN 978-1-77437-620-1 (kindle)

Subjects:
LCSH: Elephants—Juvenile literature
LCSH: Human-animal relationships—Juvenile literature

Classification: QL737.P98 L44 2020 | DDC J599.67—DC23

Contents

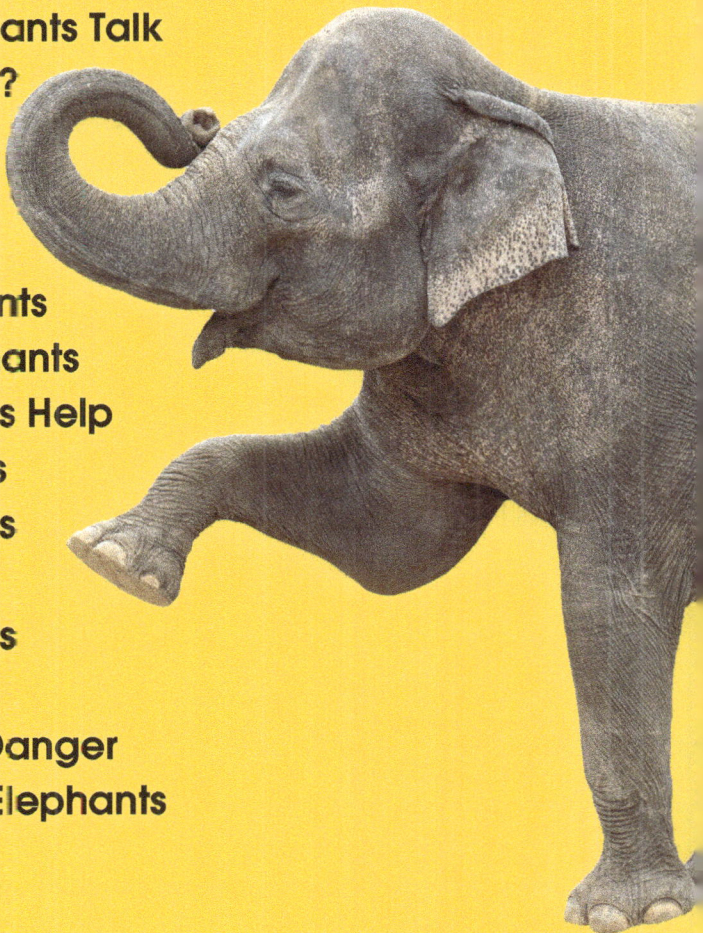

What Are Elephants?

Elephants are the largest land **mammals** on Earth. They live together in groups.

KEY WORD

Mammals: animals with warm blood and bones in their backs.

4

Elephants are thought to be one of the smartest living animals. They are helpful to people, other animals, and Earth.

A Closer Look

Some elephants can grow as tall as 13 feet (4 meters). They can weigh as much as 14,000 pounds (6,350 kilograms). That's about the same as four cars!

Elephants have big floppy ears. They can recognize voices from almost 1 mile (1.6 kilometers) away.

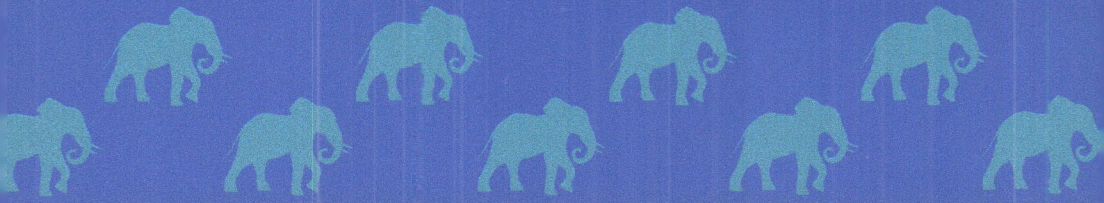

Some elephants have sharp teeth called tusks. They never stop growing.

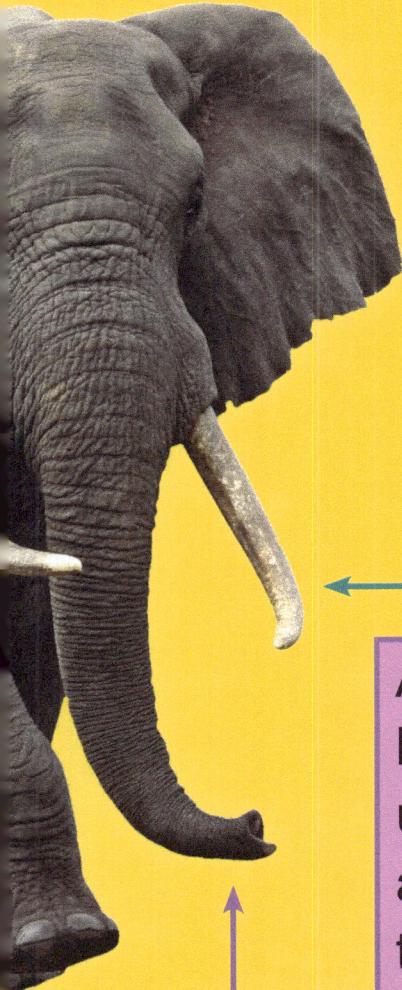

An elephant's long nose and upper lip is called a trunk. It uses its trunk like an arm to collect food.

Where Do Elephants Live?

Elephants live in many different **habitats**. They can be found in tropical forests, mountains, and grasslands.

KEY WORD

Habitats: the places a plant or animal lives. Different animals need different habitats.

Elephants live in Asia and Africa. Asian elephants are mostly found in India, Indonesia, Malaysia, Sri Lanka, Thailand, and Vietnam. African elephants can be found in most countries in Africa.

Arctic Ocean

Asia

Europe

Thailand

Vietnam

India

Africa

Pacific Ocean

Atlantic Ocean

Indian Ocean

Sri Lanka

Australia

Malaysia

Indonesia

Southern Ocean

0   2,000 miles

0   4,000 kilometers

N

Legend
Land
Ocean

Antarctica

9

What Do Elephants Eat?

Elephants eat many different plants. They often eat grass, twigs, and small bushes. One of their favourite foods is tree bark.

Elephants eat for about 17 hours every day.

Some elephants will eat dirt to gain nutrients. They dig holes in the ground with their tusks until they find the right kind of dirt. Elephants in Africa have made deep caverns by digging holes.

How Do Elephants Talk to Each Other?

Elephants trumpet, grunt, snort, and scream to let others know how they feel. Some of their sounds are so low that humans cannot hear them.

Elephants will smell and touch each other with their trunks. This helps them make friends with one another.

Elephant Life Cycle

Baby elephants are called calves. They cannot see very well when they are born. They find their mothers by smell, sound, and touch.

Male elephants leave their **herd** when they are between 10 and 14 years old. Female elephants stay with their herd their whole lives. Elephants live to be 60 to 80 years old.

KEY WORD

Herd: a group of animals that live together.

Curious Facts About Elephants

Elephants make their own sunscreen. They cover themselves in mud or dirt to prevent sunburns.

Baby elephants can stand within 20 minutes of being born.

Elephant herds are led by the oldest female in the group.

16

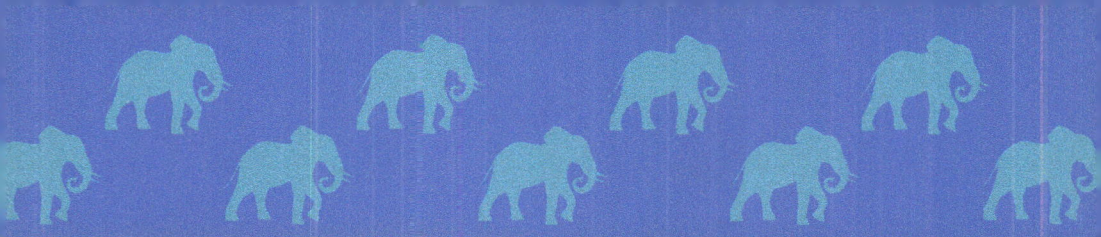

Elephants have amazing memories. They are able to remember old friends, and the best places to find food.

Female elephants can have as many as 12 babies during their lifetime.

Elephants sleep for four hours every night. Two of these four hours are spent standing.

17

Kinds of Elephants

There are three kinds of elephants. Asian Elephants live in Asia. African forest elephants and African savannah elephants live in Africa.

Asian elephants are the smallest of all elephants. They have small round ears and a dent in the middle of their heads.

African forest elephants have oval-shaped ears. Their tusks point down towards the ground.

African savannah elephants are the largest elephants. They have the biggest ears of any kind of elephant.

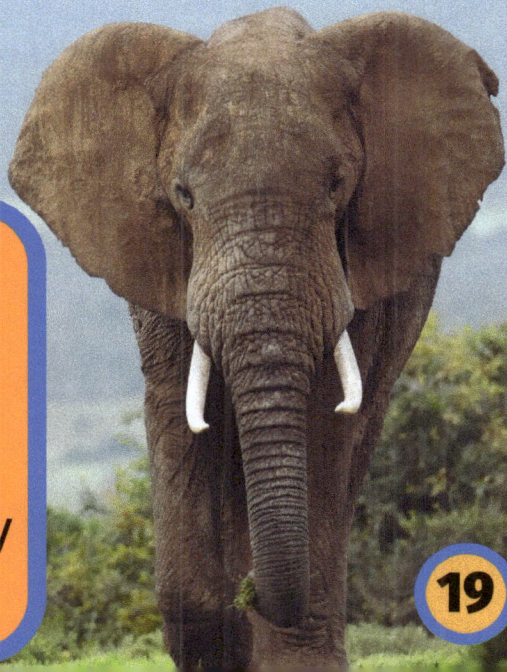

How Elephants Help Other Animals

Elephants use their tusks to dig in the ground for water when there is no other water around. This gives other animals who cannot find water a place to drink.

Elephants knock down branches, leaves, and twigs from tall trees when they look for food. Small animals are able to eat what is left on the ground.

How Elephants Help Earth

Elephants eat many kinds of plant seeds. The seeds come out in their poop. Elephants spread seeds to new areas when they travel.

22

Elephants create gaps between plants as they eat. This can let sunlight reach the ground. This helps new seeds to grow.

How Elephants Help Humans

Wild elephants are a tourist attraction in many areas. They help bring in money for local communities. These communities are then able to better protect elephants.

About one in every five humans gets **cancer**. Only one in every twenty elephants gets cancer. Scientists are studying why elephants get cancer less often. This can help them create a cure for humans.

KEY WORD

Cancer: a disease caused by cells that grow and spread too quickly.

Elephants in Danger

Asian elephants are endangered. This means there are very few of them left. African elephants are vulnerable. This means they may soon become endangered.

Elephant tusks are used in Chinese medicine to help treat illnesses. Scientists have found that elephant tusks do not work as a medicine. Some people continue to hunt elephants even though it is illegal.

How To Help Elephants

People can help elephants by adopting one. Companies who help save elephants use the money from adoptions to help protect elephants.

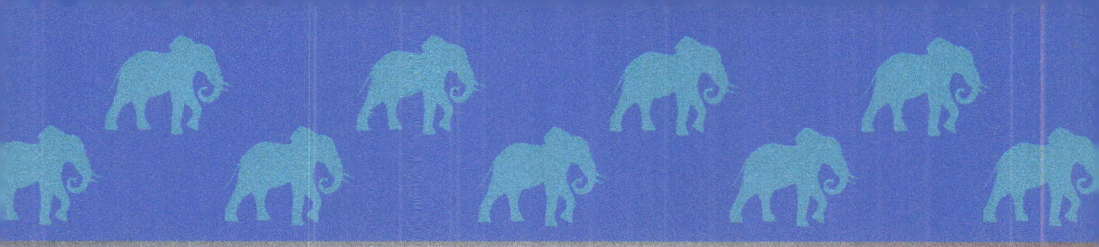

Tell your friends and family how elephants are being hunted for their tusks. Let them know that elephant tusks do not help people who are sick. More people can help save elephants if they know the dangers elephants face.

Quiz

Test your knowledge of elephants by answering the following questions. The questions are based on what you have read in this book. The answers are listed on the bottom of the next page.

1 How long do elephants spend eating every day?

2 Why do some elephants eat dirt?

3 What are baby elephants called?

4 What do elephants use for sunscreen?

5 How many kinds of elephants are there?

6 What do elephants use to dig in the ground for water?

Explore other books in the Animals That Change the World series.

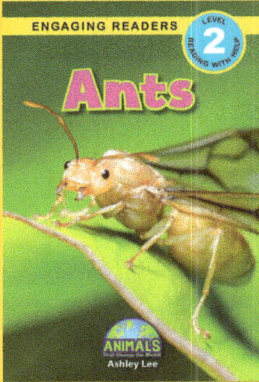

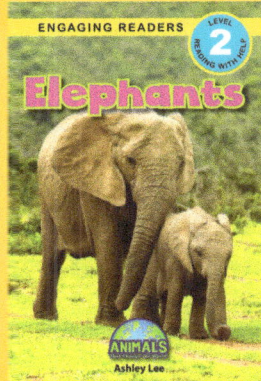

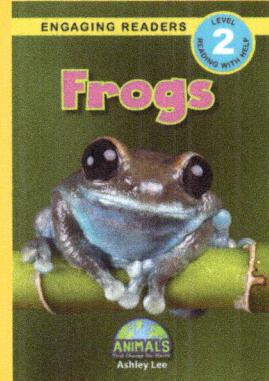

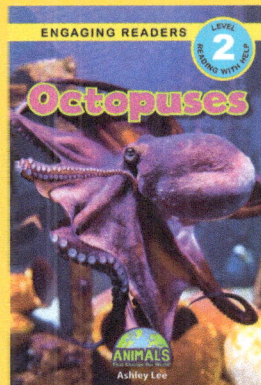

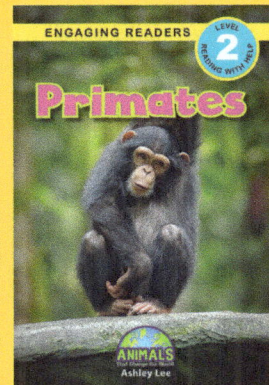

Visit www.engagebooks.com to explore more Engaging Readers.

Answers:
1. About 17 hours 2. To gain nutrients 3. Calves 4. Mud or dirt 5. Three 6. Their tusks

www.ingramcontent.com/pod-product-compliance
Lightning Source LLC
Chambersburg PA
CBHW051236020426
42331CB00016B/3396